3.95

Under Milk Float

by Martin Newell

GW00730162

The Greyhound Press

Published by the Greyhound Press in association with:
The Essex Festival
University of Essex
Wivenhoe Park
Colchester
Essex.
CO4 3SQ

Printed and bound by Essex University

Wood engravings by Barry Woodcock
Back photograph by Malcolm Latchman

By the same author:
I Hank Marvinned
(£2.50 plus A5 SAE to Essex Festival)
The Greyhound Press

This book is dedicated to Boudicca
Who burnt the cakes.....
and everything else

Hats off to....

Barry Woodcock.....	*For his generosity and talent*
Malcolm Latchman....	*For layout, design, three-day birthday celebrations...a difficult labour.*
Joe Allard....	*For educating Rita*
Giles Smith....	*A backword boy*
Annabel Llywellyn Cowper and **Roddy Ashworth...**	*Who, when I floundered in self-doubt, constantly reassured me that I was crap.*
The Barwomen at **The Greyhound...**	*Ha! Painted Jezebels.*
The Boys in the Public Bar	*"Mine's an Electric Soup"*
MoonAge Productions	*"Men in their Maytime"*

Welcome to the Three Chord Week.

Playlist

Ah Joe ...

This is my second collection of poems. Some read well and
some are more geared to performance. If you find yourself
in difficulties with them, smoke some fags and drink some
beer then mess your hair up and read them in a sloppy rock
drawl with a bit of north-east Essex in it.

I'm not very erudite. I'm such a trash-junkie. I got hold of
a copy of Michel de Montaigne's Essays but I haven't read
it yet because I was more interested in reading Ronnie
Spector's autobiography.

It was a hell of a year for me last year, what with the poems
in the papers and the media stuff and the gigs. I think I got
a bit cocky but I'm over the worst.

I've shoved rock music on the back-burner now. It's been
weird for me getting acceptance for something which I
didn't really think anyone would care about. I reckon the
reason I got obnoxious, was that the yobbo in me didn't
want anyone to think I'd gone mushy round the edges.
Anyway as Mr Sherrin said, I've put away childish things
now, so I suppose I'd better get on with being an ersatz poet
in his late thirties. Worse things could happen.

I did a couple of gigs recently, as a bass-player for The
Doors Show. Down the road to London - up the road to
Norwich ... same as I did so many times before in my late

teens and early twenties. I used to be the singer then but apart from that, it hadn't really changed. On the way back from Norwich, I even pissed in a lay-by I hadn't seen for about seventeen years. I didn't feel sad but as I sat in the shadows in the back of the van, I think I finally said goodbye to a prolonged adolescence which began with me getting my first guitar.

You'll notice a few sixties references. I got there too late and it was over by the time I was sixteen. I felt like I'd watched a really good party through the bannisters at the top of the stairs. I sometimes read about other poets. Robert Burns who left to become a customs officer and John Clare who went mad.

I think about Brian Jones and Jim Morrison and I wonder what Syd Barrett is doing now and if the past is a foreign country then I reckon I must have dual citizenship, because for good or for ill, I seem to spend a lot of time there.

Walking down Colchester High Street one hot day in August, I met the 19 year-old edition of me coming the other way. Tailcoated, kohl-eyed, barefoot and spaced-out, he said, "Well? Do I make it?" I said, "No you don't .... and put some shoes on - you prat".

Your youth is like a quay. One day you look back and you notice your boat's pulled a lot further away from it. You look through binoculars at it to see if there's anyone you recognise, but there's just a bunch of strangers queueing for the next boat and no-one's waving goodbye, so you go downstairs for a drink and hope the band plays your song. Then at night, Time, that fucking vandal, comes to slash your face while you sleep and the only thing which can save you is your sense of humour.

And I like to hang out in the public bar of The Greyhound with the brickies, the builders, the railmen, the chippies and sundry scruffbags. In the early summer, when I've been working outside all day and I'm scratched and stung and dusty, I like Tom Petty and Led Zeppelin really loud on the juke-box. And I like drinking half-Heineken with half-Special Brew because it does the job. And there's work about and will be for months - and there's some money on Friday night and the world is a shining place. And another reason I like it, is because I don't have to meet 'writers' whose word-processors are the only thing that's gone down on them recently.

Enough of this. I hope this is a good collection. If you can't get me some money, you can pay me in beer, Kalashnikovs or sheep. Aaaaand remember kids .... Image is the tee-shirt of the soul.

Martin

Your man in Essex with a
disposable lighter and a headache

Under Milk Float ... or Colchester Tales

In autumn - when fires are lit
I dream of broken fences in Cambridge Walk
Where conkers fall and spikey boys
Dog half-smoked spliffs en route to school

And by St Botolphs Circus
In Fagin's Den
I dream guitars and bullet-belted boys
And skinny girls who cry
In the amphetamine blue night

When the rain falls in Culver Street
The long-forgotten faces
From long-closed pubs
All asleep now walk beside me
Andy, Ted and Antoinette
Killed by drugs or motorbikes
Or coming home from parties
In the drunken dawn
All asleep now

In October - on Friday nights
I hear the hissing gas fires in Maldon Road
And the bedsit kids in thin black clothes
Who listen to the Mish - live on chips
Put their face on after work
Take their washing home to Mum
And spend all week in monochrome

On Scheregate steps I met the devil
Standing by the paper shop
Tired now and middle-aged
Smoking in a track-suit top

And autumn when the sky is slate
And Priory Street is misty
I dream the teenage soldiers
Kissing chubby schoolgirls
In Artillery Folley
One kiss for now
And one for the Shankhill Road

And Old King Cole
Can't claim the dole
They caught his fiddlers three
But he does alright
In the Middleborough night
With his black and white TV

In the High Street - by the Hippodrome
In the orange afternoon
I dream the oyster feast
The town council
The red carpet
For celebrities
To gorge themselves in the town hall
While some bag-lady
Goes down with reality poisoning
Outside Sloppy Joe's

In autumn - when fires are lit
I take a tea-time bus up Greenstead Road
With rabid steamy shoppers in their android clothes
Who dream of Telecom vans
And double glazing
Of shopping as religion
And cable television

Of rain-splashed windows in Lexden Road
Of half-term lovers on Hilly Fields
Of half-heard sirens in Castle Park
Of swishing car-tyres down Brook Street
And listen to me now
In autumn when fires are lit
I dream

They Also Surf.....Beach Boys tributes pour in from Essex

If Brian Wilson came from Clacton
And not the USA
He'd have a very different postcode
From Californ-I-AY
You'd find it hard to imagine
The way it might have been
Had everybody gone surfin'
CO17

Well East Coast girls are hip
I really dig those coats they wear
And the Southend girls
When they eat their chips
They knock me out when I'm down there
The Essex farmers' daughters
Wear their jodhpurs far too tight
And the Maldon girls
With the way they spit
At their boyfriends late at night
But I wish they all could be
Saffron Walden girls

Well she hasn't got a car
And you can't rely on Eastern Region
And the Frinton over- sixties surfers
Had a very poor season
And they're rather short of happening bands
At the British Legion
But she'll have Fun Fun Fun
Till her daddy takes the tea-bag away

Moon Over Colchester

Moon over Colchester
Shine down hard
The outside loo in God's back yard
Was never so divinely starred
As this town
Where soldier boys in shiny boots
Fought farmers' sons squeezed into suits
For sturdy girls of seventeen
From Fingringhoe or Eight Ash Green

Moon over Colchester
Shine down bright
The sodium halo in the night
Is not a sympathetic light for muses
But nonetheless they do appear
From time to time throughout the year
And poets grab them while they can
They don't appeal to Essex Man

Moon over Colchester
Shine on now
Tiara turned up by the plough
Bespattered by that passing cow
Called progress
The dazed commuter off his train
With mortgage fear and aching brain
Has settled in the town which grew
From some Iceni barbecue

Moon over Colchester
If you dare
Recall that stranger standing there
Was fierce of face with reddish hair
As I am
But Boudicca declined to stay

And I, her son am here today
I bear no grudge I'm pleased to say
I've lost my lighter anyway

Meanwhile - back in the studio.....

The drummer was a carthorse
He wasn't very tight
We nudged it with an a.m.s.
To get the fucker right
We mumbled something in his ear
About an overdub
Then told him he could take a break
And sent him down the pub
We couldn't rouse the bassist
He was lying on his back
We had to use a sample
Where he would have had his track
Doesn't matter-anyway
The rhythm track was sagging
Goes to show the damage done
By taking drugs and shagging
The singer was a narcissist
Who couldn't sing a note
Largely cos his tongue was firmly
Down his boyfriend's throat
The only time we ever saw
The keyboard player play
Was just before the mental nurses
Hoisted him away
The geezer who was on guitar
Was playing with some expression
Until we found he'd wandered in
From someone else's session
And as for the producer
He was hardly ever there
He listened to it once or twice

And made us gate the snare
Then buggered off to EMI
With filofax and phone
And left us here to finish off
The album on our own
So everything that's down on tape
Everything you hear
Was the product of a tape-op
And a knackered engineer

Coda
Blah blah track sheet
Have you got it mixed?
Yes sir yes sir
Almost fixed
One for the dance floor
One for your brain
And one for the little man
 Who brings the cocaine

CHAANNG

We are haunted by the sixties
The opening chord of Hard Day's Night
Hangs frozen in the cold night air
And people who were never there
Who couldn't know or didn't care
Now fall in love at second sight
As psychics looking backwards might

We are haunted by the sixties
That last weekend of sunny days
Before the winter term began
The lipstick message on the van
Has faded and the ageing fan
Now claims it was a passing phase
But stops - each time the music plays

We are haunted by the sixties
And precious youth in pointy boots
Who says his parents got it wrong
Will secretly still sing along
And knows the words of every song
But then denies he took his roots
From northern boys in Beatle suits

We are haunted by the sixties
The still-familiar faces stare
From retrospective magazines
The anthems swallowed by machines
Now re-emerge to sell us jeans
A ghostly party everywhere
We cannot join the dancers there

Smoke on the Water

In music shops on Saturdays
You'll nearly always find
The faces of assistants there
Are prematurely lined
The reason for this ageing
Is repeated aural slaughter
By amateur guitarists
Playing Smoke on the Water
In the kingdom of the riffless
It's rated as the king
And once it's in the repertoire
They won't stop playing the thing
An iron-clad example
Of a riff which gives no quarter
And the musical equivalent
Of solid brick and mortar
As popular as Stairway
But easier and shorter
An embolism-if you like
In rock and roll's aorta
It qualifies as music
But it's nothing like Cole Porter
It's Ritchie Blackmore's Frankenstein
Smoke on the Water

Dawn of a Teenage Drug Fiend

In an attic room in a leafy crescent
Something stirs which isn't pleasant
Belches, squelches, goes tumescent
Werewolf? No it's an adolescent .....

From here on in, you're on your own
It's anti-social, fully grown
It's most coherent sound's a moan
Unless of course it's on your phone
I'd hate to add to any fears
But since you're on the brink of tears
It hangs around for several years
And fills your house with all its peers
Who chip your mugs
And burn your rugs
Then steal your jugs
To mix their drugs
You'll plead, "For Christsakes - not in here!"
That's when they take it up a gear
By mixing acid, whizz and beer
To add the element of fear
And where d'you start with all of that
A bawling out? A cosy chat?
Like, "Don't give sulphate to the cat".
Or just move out and get a flat?
There's no escape - just wait and see
But slash your wrists and instantly
And if you'll take a tip from me
You'll do it while the bathroom's free.

The Fifth Dimension

I've found the fifth dimension
It's underneath my bed
It's not to do with outer space
Or anyone who's dead
It's like a kind of cupboard
But in another world
Where missing bits of cannabis
And other things get hurled
Stuff you lost at parties
Like the ten Silk Cut
You were saving for a crisis
If the pub was shut
Or a number on a Rizla
Of a woman that you met
Who was rich and owned a chemists
And was looking for a pet

I've found the fifth dimension
And now I really know
Where biro tops and single socks
And missing plectrums go
It's full of pairs of knickers
Which when they disappeared
Led to accusations
And talk that you were weird
It's similar to Narnia
But crawling with cassettes
Which vanished from their boxes
Like well-loved pets
It's Blackmail Corner
It's the Holy Grail
You'd better bring some money round
There's gonna be a sale

Virtually In Love ... Or Safer Sex with Cybernetics

Sigh no more in cyberspace
When push comes to shove
In virtual reality
You're virtually in love
Headpiece over glove
With a 3 D duchess
From your one-track mind
She's teledildonic
It won't make you blind

Well caught cybernaut
Lonesome no more
Your symphony in silicone
Is waiting to withdraw
To an opium-scented chilling chamber
Out on level four
Turn software into hardware
Turn headgames into bedgames
From missionary position
To hanging from the door
She's virtually an acrobat
But certainly no whore

You're virtually in love with her
She's virtually your girl
You're datahand-in-dataglove
A telepresent whirl
Of cybernetic smoochiness
Which virtually means
You can virtually feel it
When her hand goes down your jeans

You're virtually experienced
And barely in your teens

A lovestruck junkie
In a strange new game
A blue-chip monkey
With a red-hot dame
When you virtually undressed her
You virtually came
A cyborg stole your cherry
And you never knew her name

Return to Stepford

Stepford men Stepford wives
Stepford houses Stepford lives
Stepford motors Stepford shops
Stepford Top of Stepford Pops
Standardise, lobotomise
Always try to normalise
Blandest android gets a prize
Hence the verb, "to Stepfordise"

Buy that place, get that job
Hire that robot, fire that yob
Buy that child expensive toys
Dolls for girls, guns for boys
Stepford bath Stepford bog
Stepfordise the bloody dog
Rolled-up paper on the snout
Stops his spirit breaking out

Stepford love, Stepford marriage
Stepford freezer in the garage
Stepford girls? Dawn and Karen
Stepford boys? Wayne and Darren
Stepford mission? Stepford shopping
Education? Fortress Wapping
Any questions? Stepford silence
Quick solution? Stepford violence
Deviants? in an institution
Ridicule then brain ablution
Get them young, stop them thinking
Give them game shows-keep them drinking
Nothing Stepford needs to know
Can't be hired on video

Spending power? Quite elastic
Thanks to banks and Stepford plastic
Stepford skies are always blue
Stepford now invites you to
Come to Stepford barbecue
Wear a Shell-suit if you do
Stepford's current occupation?
Sunday Fun Run, Stepford Station
Funny noses, frilly knickers
Party later - tarts and vicars
Stepford's happy, told me so
Said on Stepford Radio
Advertising Stepford Show
Sounds like fun - I think I'll go

It's a bit like Wivenhoe

Blue-Stocking Groupie

I'm a blue-stocking groupie
That's what I said
Better dead than badly-read
Stern in study
Strong in head
Brainy birds are best in bed

I'm a blue-stocking groupie
Yeah yeah yeah
My love sits in that Big Black Chair
With tousled hair and steely stare
Answering questions on Voltaire

I only make passes
At girls in glasses
Only want sex
With women in specs
I.Q. City's where it's at
I don't want some bimbo prat
A mortar-board's a horny hat
Fwooaarr-look at the brains on that
You can do your studying round MY flat
I'm a blue-stocking groupie
And that's that

The Lone Ranger's Psychic

Sometimes
She was a radio
The voices came
Into her head
Quite randomly
And of the dead
Some she liked
And some, she said
Were tedium
Other times
The shapes she saw
Were outlines only
Nothing more
And intuition
Was a chore
Like breaking cyphers
During war
But this apart
And overall
She was
A happy medium

Tusk Tusk

Fleetwood Mac
Took some flak
Changed their line-up
Then came back
Took some risks
Mass acceptance
Was quite brisk
Heady mix
Lindsay's licks
Fleetwood's beat
And Stevie Nicks
Sexy croak
Due to smoke
Not to mention
Lots of coke
Late-ish nights
Jet-lag flights
Bound to lead
To nasty fights
First excess
Then egress
Leading to
A legal mess
When the stars
Start in bars
Then end up
In yuppy cars
Faces lined
Never mind
This is what
The famous find.

God Bless Tina Turner

God bless Tina Turner
Stuck for years on rock's back-burner
Now the sales are really soaring
But the songs are slightly boring

God bless pop's Queen Mum
Raggy dress and tassled bum
Older fellows go all trembly
When they hear she's playing at Wembley

God save the queen of thigh
Have those medics standing by
Sudden pressure in the pipes
Kills these ageing business types

God preserve Miss Annie-Mae
Craps on Cilla any day
Never seem to see old Ike
Since she sent him on his bike

Long live old Velcrose Voice
Would Wincarnis be the choice
Rather than her tea and honey
If she needed sponsor money?

Bottle of Youth

Had a bottle of youth
I carried about
I shook it up till the cork came out
I took a swig - it tasted sweet
I spilled a bit in Wardour Street
It trickled down to Leicester Square
And left a pool of memories there

Had a bottle of youth
Just laid on me
It seemed to blur mortality
Clear and good it bore my name
And all my friends got one the same
It cured fear and banished doubt
We never saw it running out

Had a bottle of youth
Gone halfway down
And drunk on it I owned the town
I knew the world and it knew me
And no change due that I could see
I wrote that riff I banged that drum
I never heard those strangers come

Got a bottle of youth
With some left still
I only take it if I'm ill
And since my friends have gone to ground
I never have to pass it round
So wiser now I watch and think
As all these strangers waste their drink.

The Little Death of Summer

Summer, mad and perfumed girl before
The honeysuckle dies at my back door
Kiss me long and soft in little death
Now I lie demolished on your floor
Baby you've got graveyards on your breath
And I don't think you love me anymore

Numb me with your opium kiss tonight
I am destroyed I have no will to fight
Bruise my lips but leave me no goodbyes
Now I risk a fever from your bite
There's only desolation in your eyes
And I don't wish to see you in the light

Thorpe Market

The bric-a-brac and gaudy tack
Of any generation
Are sold for pennies not for pounds
At Thorpe-le-Soken station
And kept in circulation

The portrait of King Edward swings
In creaking celebration
And peels by the public house
At Thorpe-le-Soken station
In which they serve libation

Then plant and flower auctions
In rusting iron sheds
Are filled with Essex faces
On weathered turnip heads
From Clacton or from Toosy
With their end-of-winter colds
Who bid at Thorpe-le-Soken
For a box of marigolds
At one pound eighty? Eighty-five?
Ninety do I hear?
They stick at one pound ninety
And sod the auctioneer
Who glances over half-moon specs
With keen and practised eye
At hardy annual gardeners
Who won't be hoist so high

And paperbacks laid up in stacks
Defying your concentration
Are found on trestles ten-a-pound
At Thorpe-le-Soken station
Some still in publication

The prices paid for literature
Immune here to inflation
Where Barbara Cartland lies with Joyce
At Thorpe-le-Soken station
For your imagination

But despite the April sunshine
There's an easterly which wields
A cutting edge to chill you
From the Thorpe-le-Soken fields
And there beneath the conker tree
In quiet resignation
The traders turn their collars up
At Thorpe-le-Soken station
And curse their occupation

The maltings by the railyard
The legend says it plain
Make malt for Double Diamond
You'll read it from the train
You can smell it in the market
You can taste it in the rain
And it lingers in your nostrils
Till you're nearly home again

Then market women's wartime eyes
Are closed in concentration
To tally takings in the pub
By Thorpe-le-Soken station
A tricky operation

And I may have a drink or two
Of devil's embrocation
I like to watch the trains go by
At Thorpe-le-Soken station
And miss my destination.

September

September sashays in
Like a hippy tart on gin
As summer staggers out
Like a grebo with the gout
The wind, a pale midshipman
And a dog with golden eyes
Run ragged up the pavement
Where a widow quietly cries
In the neo-Georgian morning
When leaves blow up the hall
And sadness stalks the suburbs
And early apples fall
Where Death does up his Burberry
And lights a mean cigar
As the dust falls softly
On a jilted girl's guitar

God

God moves in mysterious ways
His good works to perform
He periodically washes up
And sometimes mows the lawn
He takes the collie down the rec
And switches off at night
Unplugs the television
But leaves an upstairs light
When Doreen got contractions
He took her in his car
He helped your grandad
Putting in the kitchen breakfast bar
His part-time job in Tescos
Means money all the time
For ten Silk Cut, his Fruit and Nut
And bottle of barley-wine
Yes God is always with us
Insists we call him Roger
In many ways he seems to be
The better sort of lodger
Amen

Heroin in Whiskas

There's heroin in Whiskas
I'm reasonably sure
The cat's getting desperate
Pacing the floor
He hangs round the food cupboard
Waiting to score
Wild-eyed and reckless
Quick on the claw
He's sharing a needle
The cat from next door
Comes round at mealtimes
And ties-off his paw
They shoot up together
And beg me for more
Who should I turn to?
The vet or the law?

There's heroin in Whiskas
I don't think it's crack
He said he could handle it
Lying on his back
But last night the chemists
Came under attack
The only things missing
Were chocolate and smack
And some halibut oil
From the vitamin rack
He won't have the dried stuff
Which comes in a pack
If it ain't got the tincture
He reckons it's cack

There's heroin in Whiskas
And reasonably pure
He completely refuses
To go for a cure
He just lies around
Till it's time for his feed
But what makes it worse
Is the dog's taking speed.

The Devil Writes Out....

I've played the Devils music
For nearly thirty years
And recently he wrote to me
Confirming all my fears
The letter stated cordially

Dear Musician,
Due to the recession
And our company's position
Hell-On-Earth Amalgamated
(As is our tradition)
Had a heated meeting
And came to a decision,
That when you play a venue
The contract which we send you
Will have a small addition
To the prices on the menu
A snappy little slogan
We hope you like it too.
"Why Pay The Piper
When He'll Pay You?"
We ran it up the flagpole
Discovered that it flew
We never make a killing
Where a massacre will do.
We hope that you'll accept it
And minimise the fuss
Here's the new amendment
It breaks down thus;
Eighty pounds for lighting
Hundred for p.a.
You've heard of pay-to-practice?

Well this is Pay-to-Play
You have to work in London
If you want to make it big
Purgatory Enterprises
Offers you the gig.
Any of your merchandise
Sold at the event .....
We'll happily relieve you
Of twenty-five per cent
Good band, right sound
Tunes well-crafted
Wallets out, trousers down
All get shafted.
We also charge the punters
(Just to keep it level)
So Pay-to-Play
Or stay away
Best regards

The Devil

House of Carruthers

From their denim skirted mother
To their bishop-bashing brothers
The horse-wrangling East Anglian
Family of Carruthers
Were spread-buttocked stupid
Like brain-dead mounties
A cosy Cosa Nostra
From the Eastern Counties

Their entirely lumpy daughters
Went for finishing in France
Under some absurd illusion
That they'd stand a better chance
Than the neighbours dismal failures
Who'd returned from Lucy Clayton
With molar-stripping voices
And a Marry-By date on

Their eco-wasting whiskey basting
Grain - baron father
Was permanently purple-veined
In apoplectic lather
Wishing all organic farms
Could be set fire to
And seeing Bernard Matthews
As something to aspire to

They ploughed up footpaths
They scattered passers-by
They were shotgun married
At the church of ICI
Where they held thanksgiving
With their upstretched hands
For the double-headed pheasants
On their soil-knackered lands.

Gardeners Opening Time

I have no time
To dig this ground
The day's escaped
The sun's moved round
And beer won't drink
Itself I've found
I have no time
To dig this ground
This particular ground

I'm not inclined
To pull this weed
And anyway
It's gone to seed
At half past five
I feel no need
I'm not inclined
To pull this weed
This specific weed

I wouldn't like
To cut this grass
I had the time
But let it pass
I needed strength
To lift my glass
I wouldn't like
To cut this grass
The grass in question

I do not wish
To change this shirt
The landlord
Never minds the dirt
He knows I'm working
It won't hurt
I do not wish
To change this shirt
This current shirt

I have not time
I am not keen
On things which grow
Or which are green
And working on them
Seems insane
The bastards only grow again
The pub is open
I have found
I have no time
To dig this ground
Or any ground for that matter

The Stars We Were

For one night only
Showing now
Handsome bastard
Lucky cow
Whatever costs
The years incur
We can't forget
The stars we were

And was that me?
And was that you?
We're older now
The summer's through
Some trees look good
In autumn too
More trunk less leaves
But while it's true
We liked the Frankincense
And myrrh
It's the gold
We now prefer
And on one thing
We both concur
We don't return
To stars we were

Shabby stars
But brilliant then
Godlike
In the world of men
Seventeen points
Out of ten
Ego-top-up?
Just say when

It's comforting
I have to say
To see old rivals
Going grey
To watch past lovers
Put on weight
Settle for
The going rate
The cushy sell-outs
Which occur
If we forget
The stars we were

Clapton

Sometime several long-playing years ago
Before the days of paint-spray cans and trainers
Long-haired Afghan-coated fifth-form boys
With bum-fluff beards or premature Zapatas
Crept round London's streets in dead of winter
And daubed on walls and corrugated fences
     C L A P T O N I S G O D
Jimi Hendrix intervened quite cruelly
Fickle did as Fickle ever would
Changed alliance - ditched the old religion
Clapton was not God
But merely .....
Good.

To Cut a Long Story Short

After punks and prior to goths
Bank clerks clad in table cloths
Voices with the lilting bubble
Of the Q.E.2. in trouble

New Romantics were in power
Pop declared its cocktail hour
Adam Ant, Duran Duran:
"Mummy! I'm a highway-man"

When at least the fashion went
And advances had been spent
Trusty steeds returned to stables
And the cloths went back on tables

The Iron Maiden Lig

Bring your daughter
To the slaughter
Don't forget
The Perrier water
Please display
Your backstage passes
See you after
Fencing classes

Last Orders   (for Freddie Mercury)

I defy anyone tonight
Whoever drank a pint
Or found love
Or lost love
Or ever feared they might
Not to feel saddened
When your songs come on
For faces or places
In times long gone

For whatever we were
And whoever we are
When the juke-box stops
In the public bar
Nostalgia fogs
The memory's cogs
Our youth checks out
When we lose a star

A Quick Slash

You said
I'm just going upstairs
For a quick slash
How we laughed
When you came down
With your wrists all bloody

Unsuccessful Comeback Tour

You've lost your brains
I've lost my looks
Lets lose lots of money

Mr Kipling's House Rap

Burnt top
Cake shop
Not very tasty
Talkin' bout a fly
In the big bad pastry
This is jaaam tart

Bruce Forsyth Calls It Off

Impossible to see you.
To see you ...
Impossible.
Alright my love?

This Is What She's Like

She's the sunlight come
To prison cells
On frosty mornings
She's the last cigarette
Found in a forgotten raincoat
Late at night
She's a pale ghost
In a kimono
On a dusty landing
One Saturday morning
In summer when it rains
And tea is brewing downstairs
She treads on a splinter
And bleeds perfume
She's the sound of the key
In the latch at midnight
When you stop worrying
She's a kick in the shins
At a party and her handbag
Is a mystery
She's the dripping umbrella
In the kitchen
In February when the sun
Is forty watts anaemic
And taking iron tablets
She has a row of bottles
On the bathroom shelf
With strange white potions
Which smell of brilliant women
Who never got the credit

She's the telepathy between swans
Who fly upriver in pairs
Wings tipping the grey water
At dusk when summer is gone
And once a month
She's out on loan
To the moon
Careful with her

Journey To The Bottom of Your Handbag

In the land of missing Zippo
And broken cigarettes
I went with vague instructions
In search of your Lillets
Past secret bars of chocolate
And leaflets from the vets
Reminding you the time was due
To vaccinate your pets

In kingdoms of your handbag
Mysterious and old
Through wetlands of your tissues
From when you had a cold
Braved broken biscuit landslides
And Irish fifty pees
And roamed the Make-up mountains
Prospecting for your keys

Down valleys of Guarana packs
Consumed when you were tired
I sledged upon your phone card
Which long ago expired
In forests of your hairbrush
Where humans feared to go
I found a hidden treasure
A tiny bit of blow

Through caverns of your knickers
Across the cough-sweet hills
Traversing cans of hairspray
And old cystitis pills
I found a contraceptive
In half an old cheese roll
Marooned inside your handbag
The Tardis of your soul

Miss L Holden

Supposing ...
I married the girl
In the building society
Miss L Holden
Lynn ... I later found out
With her C.F.C. hair
And her strong leanings
Towards normality
With her grey suit
And her ruffy blouse
Not too high heels.
Supposing I just woke up
And found myself married to her?
How would we get on?
Could I bring myself to like,
Her Lionel Richie cassettes?
Her Jackie Collins books?
Her Daily Mail Feminism?
Her "Mrs-Thatcher-may-be
A-complete-psychopath
But-she-says-what-she-thinks"
How would I cope with
Going to Florida
For two weeks sunbathing?
What would I do
While Dynasty was on TV?
What about sex?
I expect I'd have to
Take a shower first
And ultimately
There might be a baby

Then I'd be forced
To go to the Christening
And talk with the women
About job prospects
With the men
About cars and football
The answer might be
A computer course
Then while Lynn was at home
Nursing little Lionel
I could be on the 6.15
From Colchester to Liverpool Street
In my Burton raincoat
And Hepworth suit.
Going to work in computers
Somewhere in London
And dreaming
Of doing the square lawn
Of our Barratt home
With a flymo ...
On Sundays
There would be a lunchtime pint
Or driving in the car
To her mum's
I would sensibly
Not be under-insured
Make sure of the best buys
Go to the freezer centre
Take up DIY
Be adventurous in bed
By getting some books

On the subject.
Pay Lynn little compliments
About her hair
Still give her Valentine cards
Great big ones
With a giant shiny rayon heart
And a pre-written message.
Build a shelf
For baby things
While she read a catalogue
Yes I think perhaps
I could be quite convincing
For a while
But what would happen
If I cracked?
Supposing she came home one day
And found me completely naked
In the garden
Except for a Napoleon hat?
Being wheeled round the garden
On a small trolley
Pulled by two sheep
And shouting with laughter
Or what would happen
If I turned the spare bedroom
Into the Temple of Ra
Painted symbols on the walls
Burned incense
And took strong hallucinogenics
Chanted mantras late on Thursday nights
And had spiritual experiences?

How would she cope
With monthly Sufi weekends
Or rebirthing
In our living room?
Supposing I lent the garden shed
To a French-Vietnamese lesbian
Who needed to finish her novel?
Would Lynn mind?
I think she would
Her parents
Mr and Mrs Holden
Most certainly would
They would be onto their solicitor
Like a shot
Finding out what could be done.
Police and psychiatrists might come.
Lynn would be tearful
But determined now
I'd lose my job
The two sheep and myself
The French Vietnamese lesbian novelist
We'd all be homeless
And even though
I never married Miss L Holden
From the building society
I can't forgive her for that.

The Beano Characters ... where are they now?

Minnie the Minx is now a successful lawyer in Bracknell, Berkshire. She was instrumental in helping the Greenham women fight their cause in the eighties and has written a book about it.

Of the Three Bears, only Ted is still alive. Pa Bear died of a heart attack and Ma Bear died in the obesity wing of a Sacramento hospital after gorging herself on Bangers and Mash.

Roger the Dodger got a degree in Sociology at university and worked in advertising for 5 years before starting his own p.r. firm. He now lives in Hove where he is a tory councillor.

Dennis the Menace was unemployed for years until he took up an employment training course in carpentry. He now builds adventure playgrounds in the Bristol area and helps to run a wholefood co-op.

His dog Gnasher is dead now but fathered a litter of puppies one of which lives with Dennis and his girlfriend, Beryl the Peril.

Walter dropped out of a promising academic career and became involved in drugs. He became a writer in 1985 but in March of 1990 was found dead of a drugs overdose in his parents conservatory.

Of the Bash Street Kids, Danny married Toots and they now run a greengrocers in Maidstone, Kent. Fatty is a shopsteward at British Telecom. Plug joined the merchant navy, Sidney is an electrician and Herbert works in a shoe shop. Wilfred and Spotty are heating engineers and Smiffy is a pop star in New Zealand. Teacher retired to Majorca.

Little Plum is an Indian Rights campaigner in New Mexico. Chiefy died of alcoholism in the early seventies.

Lord Snooty and his pals now run Bunkerton Castle Pleasure Park and once a year host the Bunkerton Monsters of Rock concerts.

Billy Whizz joined the RAF and was decorated during the Falklands war. He was shot down during a bombing raid over Basra,Iraq in 1991.

Biffo the Bear runs a late night burger bar on the A12 near Chelmsford called "Ah - The Very Thing". His friend Buster is an unemployed cartoon character in Witham, Essex.